BR AIR-BRAKED WAGONS

IN COLOUR David Ratcliffe

Ian Allan
PUBLISHING

First published 2014

ISBN 978 0 7110 3460 0

Published by Ian Allan Publishing
an imprint of Ian Allan Publishing Ltd, Hersham, Surrey KT12 4RG.

Printed in Bulgaria.

Visit the Ian Allan Publishing website at
www.ianallanpublishing.com

Picture Credits

Every effort has been made to identify and correctly attribute photographic credits. Should any error have occurred this is entirely unintentional.

FRONT COVER (TOP) DC 950099, a Bogie Bolster D modified for timber traffic in 1987, is pictured at Walton Old Junction Yard, Warrington in August 1988.

FRONT COVER (LOWER LEFT) Ballast Plough Van DB 993826, repainted in Loadhaul livery is seen at Tees Yard in February 1999.

FRONT COVER (LOWER CENTRE) MGR coal hopper 355124 is pictured at Liverpool Edge Hill in May 1990.

FRONT COVER (LOWER RIGHT) FJA 601997 carrying bulk whisky containers from Keith Junction is seen at Mossend Yard in July 1990.

BACK COVER FGA 601427 brings up the rear of a Garston to Seaforth Freightliner trip near Allerton East Junction in April 1995.

TITLE PAGE Corus (British Steel) No 404, a Hunslet Electric Co 0-6-0DH, shunts empty air-braked Borail wagons for reloading with new rail at Workington Steelworks in April 2005.

CONTENTS PAGE In 1988 47 BPAs (together with 54 BDAs) were modified with new raised ends and 13 steel bolsters. Recoded BMA they carried aluminium ingots from Fort William, steel billet from Scunthorpe, section from Lackenby and slab from Port Talbot and Sheffield. BMA 965044, loaded with stainless steel slabs for export from Tinsley Park Works, Sheffield, awaits unloading at Grimsby Dock in July 1992.

Contents

Introduction

British Rail's air-braked wagon fleet can broadly be divided into two groups; vehicles converted from existing unfitted or vacuum-braked stock and those built from new with air brakes. Both groups form the subject of this book, including former BR wagons that continued in use following the privatisation of the freight sector, but, other than Brake Vans, air-piped wagons together with wagons built after privatisation are not covered.

By the end of the 19th century air-braked freight stock was the standard in North America and Europe but it was not until the 1960s that such vehicles began to be built in significant numbers in Britain, initially by the private wagon builders such as Charles Roberts and the Standard Wagon Co, and then in BR's own workshops

ABOVE The 12 Highfits fitted with air brakes in 1970 were later assigned to the 'Air-Braked Network', the dedicated air-braked wagonload services first introduced in 1972, where they spent several years carrying government stores from the Royal Ordnance Factory at Glascoed. Coded OHB they could also be found loaded with railway equipment and B 489405 is seen waiting to leave Woodham's scrapyard at Barry with recovered wheelsets destined for Swindon Works in October 1982. *Hywel Thomas*

at Ashford, Doncaster, Shildon and Swindon. However, by that date BR was encouraging many of its customers to invest in their own rolling stock resulting in a resurgence in the numbers of privately-owned wagons, while BR concentrated on meeting the needs of the nationalised industries and the Armed Forces. Consequently the BR-built air-braked wagon fleet was dominated by general-purpose vehicles; along with wagons for coal and steel traffic, with far fewer specialist designs than had been constructed in earlier years.

In February 1948, a month after the creation of BR, the Railway Executive had appointed the Ideal Stocks Committee to determine the 'ideal' numbers and types of locomotives and rolling stock that would be required by the newly nationalised industry, given the likely traffic levels and anticipated efficiencies to be gained from the unification of the previously competing railway companies. As well as considering the design of future vehicles the Committee also deliberated on the use of the continuous brake on freight stock, although they were unable to come to a decision since the saving in freight train hours had to be set against the cost of equipping all or part of the wagon fleet, and it was decided that further investigation of the matter should be undertaken. However, throughout this review

LEFT Experimental air-braked van B 787395, fitted with two sliding doors per side, is pictured at Edge Hill carrying bagged fertiliser from Leith to Liverpool Canada Dock in November 1976. *D. Ratcliffe collection*

it was accepted that the 'continuous brake' was synonymous with the 'vacuum brake' and although the Committee did tacitly acknowledge the superiority of air brakes it seems by this date the railways were too far committed to even consider changing.

Indeed for the next 15 years BR continued to build both unfitted and vacuum-braked wagons to designs that had fundamentally changed little since the 1930's and which were ill equipped to compete with the growth in road transport. The increasingly parlous state of the rail industry was spelt out by Dr Beeching in 1963, but while his report is best remembered for its plans regarding wholesale passenger withdrawals it also contained a number of constructive

ABOVE The Armed Forces relied upon BR to provide the bulk of the main line rolling stock required to move military equipment around the country, and in September 1993 MoD No 252 River Sark, a 300hp Thomas Hill Vanguard class 4wDH shunts two railway-owned vans, a VGA and a VEA, at Smalmstown Depot near Carlisle.

BELOW Amongst the most successful of all the BR air-braked wagons were the bogie Freightliner flats first introduced in 1964. Class 87 No 87019 heads north with a Willesden to Holyhead working south of Rugby in spring 1975.

proposals as to how the freight service could be improved. These centred around the need to utilise the improved haulage capabilities of the recently introduced diesel and electric locomotives by increasing the number of lengthy block train workings and introducing larger wagons suitable for operation at high speed.

Although a reliable system the traditional vacuum brake required a considerable volume of air to be admitted or exhausted from the braking system which could cause problems, particularly on long trains where the vehicles at the head of the formation would respond well before those at the rear with the risk of snatching and broken couplings. A modified vacuum brake, known as Accelerator Freight Inshot or AFI, which reduced this risk, was fitted to a number of vehicles in the early 1960s. However, the superiority of the air brake, which used compressed air at a pressure up to 100psi making it more responsive particularly at higher speeds and with greater tonnages, was clearly evident. In 1963 BR constructed a fleet of dual-braked 41ft 11in long two-axle ferry vans for traffic to the Continent that were based on European practice and in 1964, the year it was decided that all newly-constructed wagons should have air brakes, the first Merry-Go-Round coal

hoppers were introduced. In 1966 a batch of long wheelbase Palvans for Ford automotive component traffic took to the rails with air brakes and after several more experimental prototypes were trialled the first production batches of air-braked opens and vans began arriving from BREL's Ashford Works in 1971. However, as the new wagons would not be able to cope with all the types of traffic on offer a significant number of older vehicles were rebuilt with air brakes including Bogie Bolsters, Boplates, Borails, Highfits, Pipe wagons, Trestles, Vanfits and Vanwides.

The majority of wagons inherited by BR upon nationalisation were given a single-character prefix ahead of their fleet number dependent on whether they had originally belonged to the LNER (E), LMSR (M), SR (S), or GWR (W). Wagons built by BR received a 'B' prefix while the single-character prefix was itself prefixed by 'D' for wagons in departmental stock. However, soon after the decision to begin building a new fleet of air-braked vehicles BR also decided to introduce a new number series for such wagons which omitted the letter prefix although in later years, when many air-braked wagons were re-assigned to the various engineers fleet they were given a 'DC', 'ADC', or 'KDC' prefix as appropriate. In 1971 BR introduced a real-time computer system to regulate its entire operations, the Total Operations Processing System, each wagon being given a TOPS code that was painted on its information panel indicating vehicle type and the automatic braking system where fitted. (See Tables 1 and 2.)

The first air-braked wagons were painted freight brown with white lettering until in 1975 a new maroon livery was introduced for opens and vans. Unfortunately, although attractive when new the maroon quickly faded to brown and so when BR re-launched its air-braked wagonload services under the 'Speedlink' brand in 1977 a new livery of flame red and grey was adopted. However, it took many years to repaint the entire wagon fleet and examples of all three liveries could still be found in 1987 when the Railfreight business underwent sectorisation. This brought yet another new livery of dark grey and yellow but relatively few wagons carried this scheme before it was overtaken by the setting up of the three shadow privatisation companies, Loadhaul, Mainline Freight, and Transrail, whose desire to establish their own identities resulted in three more liveries taking to the rails. If one also considers the special liveries carried by those open wagons modified for Plasmor and Redland traffic and the various departmental liveries, then by the 1990s the air-braked wagon fleet presented a very colourful if not particularly coherent picture.

As with my previous books in this series I must thank all those railway men and women who provided information and let me take photographs in their yards and goods depots, as well as Trevor Mann, Mark Saunders, Hywel Thomas, David Larkin and John Edser who have kindly given me access to their extensive photographic collections once again.

David Ratcliffe
Swinton
2014

Table 1

TOPS Wagon Categories – (indicated by 1st letter of TOPS code) at January 1984

Code	Description
B	Bogie Steel Carriers
C	Covered Bulk Carriers
F	Flats
H	Hoppers
I	International Ferry Wagons (Foreign registered)
J	Bogie Coil
K	Two-axle Coil
M	Minerals
O	Opens
P	Privately owned (other than Tanks)
R	Barrier and Runner Wagons
S	Two-axle Steel Carriers
T	Tanks Wagons (British Privately Owned)
U	Open Bulk Carriers
V	Vans
X	Special Wagons
Y	Bogie Departmental Wagons
Z	Two-axle Departmental Wagons

Notes: The 'J' and 'K' categories were subsequently reallocated to privately owned wagons, while the 'U' and 'X' categories were abolished. No air-braked wagons were assigned to the 'U' category.

Table 2

TOPS Brake Codes

(These comprised the 3rd letter of a wagons TOPS code.)

A	Air braked
B	Air braked with through vacuum pipe
H	Dual air and vacuum braked with vacuum AFI
X	Dual air and vacuum braked

Other brake codes letters were applicable to unfitted and vacuum braked wagons

1
Open Wagons

ABOVE The first series of 100 air-braked open wagons, numbered 100000-99, were built at BREL's (British Rail Engineering Ltd) Ashford Works in 1971. Measuring 33ft 6in over headstocks with a 20ft 9in wheelbase underframe fitted with conventional 10-leaf springs, double-link suspension and disc brakes; the body comprised six-plank three-part drop-sides and similar height ends. Delivered before the implementation of TOPS they were initially coded OPEN AB and painted in overall freight brown livery with double-arrow and ABN (Air-Braked Network) symbols. Coded OAA on TOPS 100070 awaits repair at Duddeston Wagon Shops in July 1984.

RIGHT The OAAs carried a variety of traffics including bagged china clay and round timber as well as various loads for the Ministry of Defence such as compressed air cylinders, drums of lubricating oil, and coils of barbed wire. However, they were most associated with the newsprint traffic from Corpach that saw them running sheeted to customers in Bristol, Cardiff and London. OAA 100097 is pictured at Bristol Temple Meads in March 1974. *John Edser*

TOP Amongst the less common loads carried by the OAAs were packaged briquettes of Homefire which were railed from the patent fuel plant at Three Spires, near Coventry, to coal depots across East Anglia and the south east, OAA 100014 being en route to Hove when photographed at Didcot in February 1988.

BELOW AND BOTTOM In 1987 15 OAAs were fitted with higher ends for Redland roof tile traffic and repainted in the company colours, being then used on four separate flows which saw them working from Brandon to Acton, Rugby to Totton, Stirling to Gateshead, and Tiverton Junction to Cardiff. Another modification saw 19 OAAs fitted with mesh side doors in 1999 to carry concrete blocks from Merehead Quarry to Acton and from Croft Quarry to Bow. OAA 100077 is seen in Redland tile traffic at Brandon in July 1987 while OAA 100012 was recorded at Merehead in September 2002.

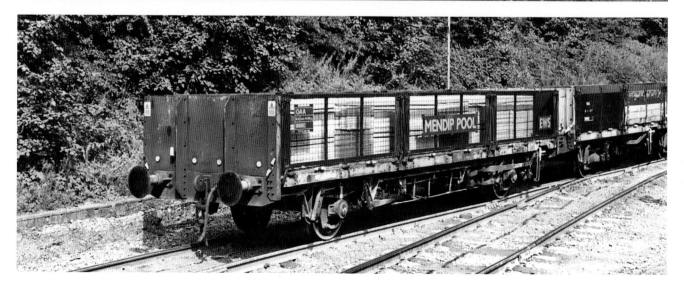

ABOVE By 1993 many of the surviving OAAs, including the Redland conversions, had been transferred to the engineers fleet and in 1996 30 were recoded ZCA after being fitted with new all steel low-sided bodies for ballast and spoil traffic. Repainted and with an 'M' prefix Mainline blue-liveried ZCA M 100093 is seen at Crewe Gresty Lane in October 1999.

BELOW In 1974 OAA 100043 was rebuilt at BREL's Shildon Works with four part drop-sides and end extensions that could be folded flat at side height. Renumbered as 110000 it was initially coded TUBE AB before becoming the first OBA and is seen loaded with concrete troughing at Castleton in April 1998.

ABOVE A production batch of 800 OBAs, numbered 110001-800, followed from Ashford and Shildon built between 1977 and 1979 with rigid ends. Like the OAA the OBA design featured removable side stanchions between the doors, those on the OBA being extendable to match the height of the ends, while the floor of the OBA was fitted with six turnover bolsters. Although retaining the 20ft 9in wheelbase the OBAs were 34ft 3in over headstocks and in 1979 the conventional suspension was superseded by Bruninghaus springs suitable for 75mph running. In 1982 the first 500 OBAs were transferred to the engineers fleet with the name BASS and recoded ZDA.

DC 110237, loaded with timber sleepers from Ditton Creosoting Depot, was photographed at Ellesmere Port in April 1985.

BELOW In revenue traffic the OBAs carried numerous commodities including aluminium billets, bagged fertiliser, rod coil, round timber and steel tubes. OBA 110752, painted in Speedlink red and grey livery, had recently arrived with a sheeted load of steel tubes from British Steel's Corby Tubeworks when recorded at Warrington Dallam Freight Depot in August 1987.

TOP In 1986 36 OBAs were fitted with end extensions and additional lashing points for the carriage of Plasmor building blocks from Knottingley and Heck to Bow and Biggleswade. Subsequently many were repainted in Plasmor colours including 110535 pictured at Biggleswade in July 1989.

MIDDLE A less successful conversion involved OBA 110793 which was fitted with high ends and an unusual peaked 'Structureflex' sliding hood at Cardiff Cathays Wagon Shop in 1985. Recoded OEA initial trials saw it carrying waferboard from Dalcross and wood pulp from Methil Docks before being allocated to the reeled paper traffic from Corpach. However, the hood mechanism proved prone to damage and by October 1994 it was to be found stored out of use at Tees Yard.

BELOW With the introduction of air-braked steel carrying wagons, such as the BDA and BRA, there was a need for compatible runner wagons and in the 1980s 71 OBAs were converted into RRAs by removal of the bodywork and fitting additional weight to the floor. RRA 110603, marshalled between two BDAs carrying overhanging steel section en route from BSC's Shelton Works to Tees Dock, is seen at Tees Yard in July 1997.

TOP AND MIDDLE Commencing in 1991 over 120 OBAs were rebuilt with new low-sided steel bodies to carry ballast and spoil. Recoded ZCA they were given the departmental fleet name SEA URCHIN, the first being delivered in the Civil Engineers yellow and grey livery although from 1995 new conversions carried the liveries of the Trainload Freight companies. DC 110242 had just been rebuilt when recorded at Marcroft Engineering, Stoke in June 1992, while T 110166, converted for Transrail in 1995, is seen at Swindon Freight Depot in December 1997.

BOTTOM For the third design of air-braked two-axle opens, numbered 112000-399, BR adopted an all steel body with three doors per side, removable side stanchions between the doors and turnover bolsters in the floor. Built at Shildon in 1981/82 the OCAs were the same length as the OBAs but all had Bruninghaus four-leaf spring suspension from new and were painted flame red. Revenue loads included bricks from Bangor, Butterly and Plymouth and rod coil from Sheerness while 69 OCAs were allocated to UKF Fertilisers at Ince & Elton from where they carried one-tonne 'Big Bags' to the firms distribution depots around the country. OCA 112297 was one of eight loaded with fertiliser for Carmarthen when photographed waiting to leave Ince & Elton in November 1984.

ABOVE AND RIGHT From 1984 over 150 OCAs were transferred to the various engineers departments and KDC 112223 had been repainted in the colours of the Signal & Telegraph Department and recoded ZDA when photographed at Stoke in May 1992. Twenty-six former OCAs were allocated to the Chief Mechanical & Electrical Engineers department including ADC 112023, one of two repainted in Railstore green and grey livery, which was spotted at Warrington Bank Quay in September 1986 when en route from BREL, Crewe Works to Longsight T&SRMD.

OPPOSITE TOP In 1987 BR introduced a new dark grey and yellow livery for revenue stock although only a handful of wagons would be repainted before the establishment of the Trainload Freight companies. These included three OCAs used to carry wheelsets from St Blazey to the wheel lathes at Carlisle Currock and Cardiff Canton. Lettered 'TO WORK BETWEEN/CARLISLE CURROCK/09191/ AND/ST. BLAZEY/85221', OCA 112232 is seen at Carlisle Currock in May 1992. The numbers 09191 and 85221 were the five-digit TOPS location codes for the C&W, Carlisle Currock and the C&W, St Blazey respectively.

OPPOSITE BOTTOM In 1989 31 OCAs were recoded ZCA and named SEAHORSE after their doors were replaced by low fixed-sides. Intended for ballast and spoil they were initially assigned to the Southern Region but by November 1998 DC 112110 was to be found at Crewe Gresty Lane.

ABOVE AND BELOW A few OCAs were repainted in the Trainload Freight company liveries including 112307, pictured with a military load destined for Marchwood, which is seen waiting to leave Bicester in June 1999 and DC 112398, spotted at Crewe Gresty Lane engineers yard in October 1999. Note the vehicle has retained its 'DC' prefix despite returning to its original OCA code.

LEFT AND BELOW As the long wheel-based open wagons could not negotiate curves of less than two chains, which were to be found inside a few military bases, BR improvised by fitting air brakes to some existing short wheel-based vehicles and in 1983 50 12-ton vacuum-braked Pipe wagons were converted at Shildon being renumbered as 113000-49 and recoded from SOV to ODA. They were used to carry crated equipment and munitions such as missiles and torpedoes that were difficult to load into a van, although precise details of their lading was often difficult to establish as they were one of the wagon types for which TOPS access was restricted. When carrying highly dangerous loads the ODAs would invariably be sheeted, 113046 being photographed at Westbury in February 1985 whilst running between the naval depots at Dean Hill and Bedenham, while 113005, loaded with crates containing aviation fuel cylinders, is pictured at Warrington Dallam in April 1990.

RIGHT Following the demise of the Speedlink network in 1991 the ODAs were recoded ZDA and transferred to department traffic. One of 12 then assigned to the timber sleeper traffic from Ditton, KDC 113020 awaits repair at Chester Wagon Shops in April 1995.

ABOVE AND BELOW Amongst the other BR air-braked open wagons were the 20 Ferry Tubes and 40 Ferry Highs built for Anglo-Continental traffic in the 1950s (see International Train Ferry Wagons in Colour for the Modeller and Historian by David Ratcliffe, published by Ian Allan, 2009). After their cross-channel workings ceased in the 1970's the Ferry Highs carried domestic traffic on the Air Braked Network, 27 of them being reduced in height from eight to five planks. Coded from OIX to OJX they handled various loads including agricultural lime from Ferryhill, military stores from Glascoed, paper from Corpach and whiting from Beverley but by the 1990s they had been relegated to departmental service. Recoded ZGA DB 715037 was spotted at Warrington in April 2000 while ZXB KDB 715002 had been converted to a crane wagon for the S&T when recorded at Healey Mills in November 1996.

2
Vans

ABOVE AND LEFT Built with two central sliding-doors at Ashford and Shildon between 1971 and 1974 were the 225 COV CDs, numbered 200325-549, which were primarily intended for the tinplate traffic from South Wales to the Metal Box factories at Aintree, Arbroath, Carlisle, Cuxton, Neath, Sutton-in-Ashfield, Westhoughton, Wisbech and Worcester. Like the COV ABs the COV CDs, which became VCAs on TOPS, could carry 29.5 tonnes but with only a 16ft wide door opening they were less versatile than other air-braked vans and in the 1980s many had the bodies removed for conversion to coal container wagons or were transferred to the engineers. Recoded ZRA and repainted in Civilink livery DC 200514 was loaded with locomotive parts when photographed at Warrington in March 1989 while DC 200511, recorded at Bescot in May 1990, carried ancillary equipment used with BR's small fleet of Bridge Beam wagons.

ABOVE The first production batch of long-wheelbase air-braked vans was based on the experimental van B 787395 with two sliding-doors per side. Initially coded COV AB 200000-324 were built at Ashford between 1969 and 1971 while 200550-649 were built at Shildon in 1974/75. The first 208 vans, which had UIC double-link suspension, became VABs on TOPS while those with BR long-link suspension should have been recoded VBA or VBB although some vehicles were incorrectly branded. Over the years these vans carried a myriad of different commodities including automotive components, breakfast cereals, bagged cement, fertiliser, kegged beer, petfood and paper, as well as tins of soup and powdered milk. They were also regularly seen in military traffic carrying everything from explosives to medical supplies and uniforms. The 20 vans numbered 200100-19 had a bonnet ventilator in each end, but no evidence has come to light that they were designed for a particular traffic, 200106 being in commercial explosives traffic from Gathurst when spotted at Warrington in June 1985. Having been repainted in Railfreight red and grey during 1983 it had recently been recoded from VAB to VAA with the removal of its vacuum through pipe.

MIDDLE AND RIGHT A number of different experimental suspensions were trialled on vans numbered in the range 200210-39, VBA 200213 being one of five fitted with FAT 8, know also as DOD MkII suspension, while VBB 200227 was one of eight with FAT 5 Taperlite suspension. Many of these experimental vans were also to be found in commercial explosives traffic, both being recorded at Wigan Springs Branch in April 1985.

ABOVE In 1990 15 former VCAs were recoded ZYA after being fitted with lighting, steps, grab rails and internal timber baulks for the carriage of concrete troughs to work sites on behalf of the Southern Region's electrification department. When LDC 200477 was photographed in September 1993 all 15 were in store at Whitemoor Yard, but by 1996 three of these unusually-liveried vans had returned to revenue service to assist with the seasonal movement of seed potatoes from Scotland to southern England.

MIDDLE Although similar in size to earlier designs the VDA featured a pair of 8ft 2in wide central sliding-doors flanked by pairs of 4ft 1in cupboard-doors at each end of the side and between 1975 and 1978 some 750, numbered 200650-201099 and 210100-399, were built at Ashford and Shildon. Until March 1987 126 VDAs, along with 12 VBBs, handled confectionery traffic from the Rowntree factories at Coxlodge and York to the companies distribution depots across the country. All had white painted roofs to help keep the product cool while 200987, one of the 20 vans numbered 200980-99 fitted with clasp rather than disc brakes, was insulated and repainted in an experimental overall white livery. It is pictured at York in May 1983. *Trevor Mann*

BOTTOM VDAs were also used for the newsprint traffic from the Wiggins Teape paper mill at Corpach. Painted in the short-lived maroon livery 210350 waits unloading at South Lambeth Freight Depot in April 1979. *Trevor Mann*

ABOVE By the mid-1980s many VDAs had been repainted in red and grey as illustrated by 210115 seen at Manchester's Ardwick West Freight Depot in February 1986. Despite still sporting hazard warning labels from a previous working, when it had carried military explosives, on this occasion it was loaded with nothing more dangerous than 38 rolls of locally produced hessian destined for the BREL carriage works at Wolverton.

BELOW A few vans were repainted with a much lighter shade of grey including 201021, one of 100 VDAs numbered 201000-99 that were built at Shildon with Taperlite suspension. When photographed at Dumfries in March 1989 it was being used as a barrier wagon for the movement of commercial explosives between the Nobel Explosives works at Annan and the ICI factory at Maxwelltown.

ABOVE Built at Ashford in 1976 with BR Friction-link suspension, 200922 was one of a pool of four VDAs used to carry whisky from the Chivas bottling plant at Dalmuir Riverside to the bonded stores in Elgin and Keith. Having been repainted in an experimental Railfreight Distribution livery the previous year it was spotted at Mossend in July 1990. Note the 'CLV' number indicating a 'Crown Lockfast Vehicle', a common marking on wagons carrying bonded traffics such as whisky.

BELOW VDA 210143 had recently been repainted in the new Railfreight dark grey livery when recorded at Warrington in August 1989. Like the earlier air-braked vans the VDAs carried a variety of commodities, although by this date they were mostly to be found in cider traffic from Hereford and Taunton and sugar beet pulp nut traffic from East Anglia, while a pool of 77 VDAs, fitted with modified floors, remained in car parts traffic between Dagenham, Halewood and Bridgend.

TOP In 1980 VDA 201070 was used to test a new door locking mechanism before being completely rebuilt with gull-wing sides in 1982, these comprising a solid lower panel with the framework above covered by a plastic curtain. Recoded VHA the vehicle was tested in paper traffic from Felixstowe Dock and with bagged fertiliser from Aberdeen and Leith but it was not a great success and, following a period in store, was converted into an OTA in 1988. It is pictured at the J. G. Russell private terminal at Aberdeen in August 1984. *Trevor Mann*

MIDDLE To expedite the movement of locomotive and wagon spares via the Speedlink network a number of VDAs were recoded ZRA and transferred to the Chief Mechanical & Electrical Engineers in the early 1980s. ADC 200654, which worked from Motherwell Carriage & Wagon Shops, is seen sporting an unusual livery at Millerhill Yard in March 1989.

BELOW From 1989 several VDAs were converted into match wagons to replace the elderly collection of opens and Brake Vans previously used to accompany London Underground rolling stock when running over BR metals. One of the initial batch of 10 vans, recoded REA, for workings to the BREL workshops at Crewe and Derby, 200756 is seen at West Ruislip in April 1993. Note the tube stock compatible coupler fitted to one end.

LEFT The refurbishment of Circle and Metropolitan line stock at the RFS works in Doncaster saw four more VDAs modified as match wagons in 1991. These were recoded RLA and 200759 was also recorded during a visit to the London Underground depot at West Ruislip in April 1993.

BELOW AND BOTTOM A second batch of four RLAs was introduced in 1992 to accompany newly built Central Line and Waterloo & City Line stock on their delivery journey from ABB Derby while, in 1995, a further four REAs, all repainted in Mainline livery, were introduced for the movement of A60 underground stock due for refurbishment at Bombardier Prorail's Horbury Junction works. Pictured at West Ruislip in April 1993 is RLA 210369 while REA 200956 passes through Didcot in April 1997.

ABOVE AND BELOW In the 1990s the British Rail Telecommunications unit was involved in the laying of fibre optic cable alongside the railways right of way. Based in Leeds, Preston and Sheffield the unit operated a small fleet of former VDAs including ZXA BDC 210274, photographed at Crewe Gresty Lane in August 1998 after conversion to a generator van, and ZDA BDC 210258, one of 17 former VDAs modified to carry concrete troughs, which was spotted at Longport in October 1994.

ABOVE AND BELOW In 1985 32 VDAs were converted into ZEA runner wagons with the removal of the body and the addition of extra weight to the floor, all being allocated to the Civil Engineer with the code name BREAM, while after the demise of the Speedlink network in 1991 over 300 VDAs were converted into low-sided ZCA departmental opens named SEA URCHIN. ZEA DC 210218 is seen at Gloucester in April 1991, while ZCA DC 200686 was spotted at Tonbridge West in June 1994.

TOP AND MIDDLE Between 1977 and 1983 550 vacuum-braked 12-ton Vanwides were air-braked, and fitted with new single-link FAT19 suspension and renumbered as 230000-549. Like the ODA conversion they were used for military traffic although the vans carried a wider range of stores and explosives such as ammunition boxes, artillery shells, hand and smoke grenades, mortar bombs, fire extinguishers, tins of paint and vehicle tyres. Initially all were coded VEA but, in 1984, 25 vans assigned to the Royal Ordnance Factory at Chorley were fitted with internal alarms and recoded VFA. Like all wagons in explosives traffic they were subject to frequent maintenance and VFA 230005 awaits attention at Ashton Road Carriage & Wagon, Manchester, in April 1986 while VEA 230489, one of a handful to be repainted in dark grey and yellow, is seen at Carlisle Currock Wagon Shop in May 1992.

BELOW When first introduced the VGAs took over the Spillers pet food working from Paisley to Wisbech, which had previously been carried in VDAs, as well as the Kelloggs breakfast cereal traffic from Barton Dock to distribution depots in Crawley, Gidea Park and Hatfield, that had previously been handled by VBAs. Two VGAs await unloading at Railstore, Gidea Park in May 1983. The 'Railfreight' and 'Speedlink' boards fixed to the sides of the VGAs would be removed in later years. *D. Ratcliff collection*

ABOVE In 1987 VGA 210418 was fitted out as a display vehicle for the Stafflink Exhibition Train complete with video equipment and seating. It is pictured at Didcot in March 1990 when on exhibition duty for the Railfreight Coal Sector.

BELOW Prior to the demise of Speedlink the VGAs had seen little use in military traffic but in 1992 186 were allocated to the MoD's nationwide pool. By that date they had also gained yellow ends, 210613 being recorded at Workington whilst en route from the Royal Naval depot at Broughton Moor to the NATO store at Glen Douglas in May 1992.

THIS PAGE In 1998 several VGAs were adorned with customer liveries and 210622, one of the two to carry Lovat Spring transfers, is seen at Blackburn freight depot shortly after arriving from Inverness with bottled mineral water in March 1999. Others included 210420, which was lettered for the Iggesund board mill, and 210579 that carried a 'Gi' logo, both being pictured at Warrington in April 1998 and August 1999 respectively when also in mineral water traffic. In all 251 VGAs were built at Shildon in 1982 numbered 210400-650. At 42ft 1in over head stocks with a 29ft 6in wheelbase their two sliding doors per side provided a loading opening of 20ft 8in by 7ft 2in.

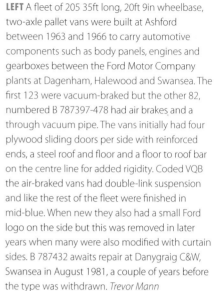

LEFT A fleet of 205 35ft long, 20ft 9in wheelbase, two-axle pallet vans were built at Ashford between 1963 and 1966 to carry automotive components such as body panels, engines and gearboxes between the Ford Motor Company plants at Dagenham, Halewood and Swansea. The first 123 were vacuum-braked but the other 82, numbered B 787397-478 had air brakes and a through vacuum pipe. The vans initially had four plywood sliding doors per side with reinforced ends, a steel roof and floor and a floor to roof bar on the centre line for added rigidity. Coded VQB the air-braked vans had double-link suspension and like the rest of the fleet were finished in mid-blue. When new they also had a small Ford logo on the side but this was removed in later years when many were also modified with curtain sides. B 787432 awaits repair at Danygraig C&W, Swansea in August 1981, a couple of years before the type was withdrawn. *Trevor Mann*

LEFT AND BELOW Ashford Works also built 250 of the 400 two-axle dual-braked ferry vans introduced by BR between 1962 and 1964 for cross-channel traffic. With the balance built by Pressed Steel all were 41ft 11in over headstocks with a 26ft 3in wheelbase, having a single 13ft sliding door and four sliding shutter ventilators each side. Originally numbered GB 786873-787022 and 787098-787347 they also had 12-digit UIC numbers but these were removed after their withdrawal from ferry service in the early 1980s. Subsequently 150 were recoded from VIX to VJX for military stores traffic before becoming barrier wagons or stores vans for the engineers. KDB 786939 had been transferred to the S&T department and recoded ZRX when recorded at Newport in September 1990, while ZQX DB 787297 was part of the North Wales Tunnel Inspection Train when spotted at Chester in April 1995.

ABOVE AND BELOW In 1977 28 BR ferry vans were renumbered 21 70 2196 000 to 027, after being fitting with curtain-sides at Ashford Works to carry motor car components from the Longbridge and Cowley plants to British Leyland's factory at Seneffe in Belgium via the Harwich Train Ferry. Previously GB 786997, the last of the batch VIX 21 70 2196 027-3 is seen at Temple Mills in August 1979. When the working to Seneffe ceased in 1983 the curtain-sided bodies were removed and the wagons converted into bogie carriers for the CM&EE. Recoded ZVX ADB 787302 (which had been 21 70 2196 021-6) was spotted at Radyr in September 1991. *Trevor Mann (1)*

ABOVE BR also owned a small fleet of 30 ferry-fitted dual-braked two-axle Covered Carriage Trucks and four bogie Scenery Vans for cross-channel traffic. Built at Lancing in 1958 the 30 14-ton capacity ferry CCTs initially handled parcels traffic and the export of expensive motor cars to the Continent but by 1983 all had been removed from ferry service and after a few years as barrier wagons they were transferred to the engineers. Coded ZQX DB 889011, previously numbered 21 70 2199 011-4, was lettered 'TO BE WORKED WITH VIADUCT INSPECTION UNITS ONLY' when spotted at Chester C&W in April 1995.

LEFT The four ferry Scenery Vans were also built at Lancing in 1958/59 with two pairs of doors each side. Like the ferry CCTs they had end doors and are also known to have carried Rolls Royce motor-cars from Crewe to the Continent, while in the 1970s one operated a monthly circuit between Manchester International Freight Terminal and Cologne loaded with groupage traffic (a mixed load of small consignments). Withdrawn from ferry service in 1981 two saw further use on the Southern Region carrying 'BRUTE' parcels trolleys to New Cross Gate for repair, while the other two had the job of delivering new platform seats from Stewarts Lane. Last of the four, 21 70 2397 003-1, also numbered B 889203, is pictured at South Lambeth in February 1979. *Trevor Mann*

TOP AND MIDDLE In 1970 BR air-braked 19 Palvans and Vanfits fitting them with single long-link suspension. Five worked from Bedford with printed materials (including Readers Digest magazines) while the others handled military traffic from Glascoed but none remained in revenue traffic by 1982. Former VPB Palvan B 781763 was in use as a generator van with the Railfreight Exhibition Train when photographed at Theale in April 1990, while Vanfit ADB 781595 was one of five former VVBs reassigned to Railstore traffic on the Southern Region when spotted at Dover Town Yard in October 1988.

BELOW In 1985 the five Mk1 Bullion Vans were transferred to freight stock and coded VXX. Three were used as mess/tool vans while M 99201 and E 99204, renumbered 889301 and 889302 respectively took up escort coach duty accompanying consignments of highly dangerous military cargoes. VXX 889302 is seen at Radyr yard in August 1991.

3
Timber Wagons

ABOVE In the 1980s round timber traffic from forests in north-east Scotland and the West Highlands began running to paper and board mills in England and Wales. Initially the logs were carried in standard OAA, OBA and OCA opens but in 1985 BR began converting 126 OCAs into OTA timber wagons, the first 50 having rectangular end extensions and 11 stanchion pockets in place of the sides. OTA 112323, carrying timber from Huntly to Hereford, is seen at Warrington in August 1997.

LEFT The other 76 initial OTA conversions had higher ends with angled top corners and most were fitted with 13 stanchion pockets per side, as illustrated by 112372 photographed at Warrington Dallam in April 1986. En route from Elgin this wagon had been stopped with a shifted load, part of which had been removed at Dallam Freight Depot before the rest could be made secure and the wagon allowed to continue its journey to Shotton Paper at Dee Marsh.

ABOVE Twenty-five more high-ended conversions were introduced in 1987. Painted blue they had nine stanchions pockets each side and were initially used to supply Thames Board Mill at Workington but, by the mid-1990s they, like all the other OTAs, were in a common nationwide pool. En route from Arrochar & Tarbet to the Kronsospan board mill at Chirk 112286 is pictured at Warrington in June 2001.

BELOW In 1992 the OTAs in traffic to Shotton began to be repainted with green ends as illustrated by 112226 photographed waiting to leave Exeter Riverside Freight Depot in September 1993.

TOP AND MIDDLE Early in 1988, to cope with additional timber traffic from East Anglia, South Wales and the South of England, 45 VDAs plus the single VHA were also converted into OTAs and the following year 32 of these new conversions were repainted in Kronospan livery to coincide with the opening of their private siding at Chirk. OTA 210193 had just been loaded at Brandon in August 1990 while the former VHA, in rather faded condition, was spotted at Dee Marsh Sidings in August 1997. By this date the Kronospan liveried OTAs were in general use and 201070 was loaded with timber from Inverurie for Shotton Paper.

LEFT An additional OTA conversion in October 1988 saw ex-VDA 200944 fitted with six curved stanchions each side, the first of an intended 30 for Forestry Commission traffic to the Caledonian Paper Co at Irvine. In the event it proved to be a one-off and is seen at Warrington en route from Crianlarich to Chirk in August 1997.

OPPOSITE PAGE In 1997 a further 71 VDAs were converted into OTAs by EWS along with 22 OBAs, the OBA conversions having similar ends to the modified OCAs while all had stake-shaped side stanchions. Empty OTA 200767 passes through Chester station in April 1998 while ex- OBA 110319 is pictured at Warrington with timber from Fort William for Pontrilas in August 1999.

4
Hoppers and Mineral Wagons

ABOVE Most numerous of all British Rail's air-braked wagons were the 32 ton Merry-Go-Round hoppers of which 11,161 were built at Ashford, Darlington and Shildon between 1964 and 1982. Fitted with automatic door-operating mechanisms they revolutionised the transport of coal to power stations and other industrial customers such as steel and cement works. When photographed at Margam in September 1990 HAA 351239, one of over 200 fitted with top canopies to increase cubic capacity, was carrying imported coal destined to British Steel at Llanwern. In 1991 vehicles fitted with canopies were recoded as HCAs.

LEFT Initially the MGR hoppers were delivered with the body framing painted brown but from 1979 this changed to flame red. HAA 355124, carrying Columbian coal from Liverpool Gladstone Dock to Fidlers Ferry power station, is seen at Edge Hill Wapping Sidings in May 1990.

ABOVE In addition to coal traffic a few HAAs were utilised as tail-lamp barrier wagons on air-braked oil trains, the last such use from Lindsey Refinery at Immingham and Coryton Refinery at Thames Haven ending in 1985. Still lettered 'OIL TRAIN BARRIER WAGON/RETURN TO/THAMES HAVEN - GRAYS E.R.', 352973 awaits cutting up at Trafford Park in February 1993.

MIDDLE AND BOTTOM In 1988 MGR hoppers began being repainted with yellow frames and a Railfreight coal sector logo, while from 1995 vehicles allocated to Mainline Freight received blue framing. Rebodied HAA 356787 is seen at Foxton in March 1991 having arrived with Polish coal from Kings Lynn Docks for Rugby Cement's Barrington Works, while HMA 356900 was spotted in the Brunner Mond Sidings at Northwich in August 1997 having recently arrived from Daw Mill Colliery, the HMA code indicating a wagon fitted with modified brakes to permit 60mph operation.

ABOVE Several other modifications to members of the MGR fleet were tested over the years including the use of aluminium alloy bodies and pneumatically operated door gear while three HAAs, 353163/320 and 355164, had their bodies cut-down for trial use carrying spent ballast. Allocated the Engineers fleet name COALFISH newly modified 353320 is seen at Burton-on-Trent in April 1994.

MIDDLE AND BOTTOM As built the MGR hoppers were restricted to 45mph but the final 460 were fitted with larger brake cylinders from new for 60mph running. Coded HDA they regularly worked in Speedlink services from Bolsover and Rufford collieries to Blue Circle Cement at Claydon and Westbury, as well as from Gedling Colliery to the government sidings at Aldermaston. Numbered 368000-459 the HDAs had the brake distributor mounted on top of the headstock. In 1991 most HDAs were recoded HBA after being fitted with top canopies for use on long-distance coal trains from Scotland to the power stations at Drax and Fidlers Ferry. HDA 368164 is pictured at Tinsley Yard in June 1985 while 368192 waits to return to traffic at Stoke after conversion to a HBA in October 1991.

ABOVE AND BELOW To serve locations where the provision of expensive MGR unloading equipment could not be justified between 1975 and 1979 BR built a fleet of 32-ton air-braked domestic coal hoppers numbered 360000-1998 (the last two underframes from the projected 2,000 being reallocated for the construction of prototype MFA scrap wagons). All the domestic coal hoppers were coded HBA until 1981 when the final 198, which had been built with Bruninghaus springs for 75mph operation, were recoded HEA. At the same time it was decided to replace the BR friction leaf suspension fitted to the rest of the fleet with Bruninghaus springs which would eventually result in all becoming HEAs. Most were delivered in freight brown while the first 221 had centrally positioned end ladders. HBA 361029 is pictured at Falkland Junction, Ayr, in August 1981 while re-sprung and recoded 360094 was spotted at Tees Dock in October 1999.

ABOVE From 1979 the HEAs began to be repainted red and grey and in 1985 150 were embellished with a St Andrew's cross to distinguish their use on traffic from South Wales to Scotland. Loaded with phurnacite from the National Smokeless Fuels palnt at Abercwmboi HEA 360731 was en route to Dundee coal depot when spotted at Warrington in June 1985.

LEFT The decline in demand for domestic coal resulted in 131 HEAs having their bottom doors sealed in 1987 and transferred to scrap metal traffic but a recoding to HSA was the only visible change from trackside, while the standard HEA were also increasingly used for other commodities including calcified seaweed from Cornwall and rock salt from Cheshire. Recently repainted 361579 waits in Warrington Arpley yard for the start of the rock salt season from the ICI siding at Over & Wharton during August 1989. Note the more convenient location of the end ladder towards the left-hand side of the headstock.

TOP AND MIDDLE In 1995 45 HEAs were refurbished and repainted in Tranrail grey becoming a common sight in 'Enterprise' wagonload service along the West Coast main line, while 44 HEA reassigned to carry industrial coal from Gascoigne Wood to Bolsover Coalite Works gained Mainline Freight livery. 361555 is seen at Warrington in April 1996 while 361124 was spotted at Marcroft Engineering, Stoke in September 1997.

BELOW The job of moving nuclear flasks to the British Nuclear Fuels Ltd reprocessing plant at Sellafield fell to the Coal Sector in 1987 and a pool of 38 HEAs were allocated for use as barrier wagons on such workings. In 1989 the hopper bodies were removed from 32 of these wagons that were then recoded RNA. They remained in barrier service until 1999 when BNFL's own PFA wagons took over the task and RNA 361581 is seen at Crewe Gresty Road in March 1993.

LEFT Although BR built no more air-braked hopper wagons in 1993 they purchased 171 redundant two-axle PGA aggregate and salt hoppers from Procor. All were then modified with cut-down bodies and repainted in yellow and grey livery for ballast and spoil traffic. After renumbering they were initially coded ZFA but in 1999, after fitting with heavy duty axle-boxes, most returned to the revenue fleet as HGAs including 390531 (formerly PR 14107), which is seen leaving Marks Tey as part of the daily sand train to Hayes & Harlington in July 2000.

MIDDLE AND BELOW Between 1988 and 1993 Doncaster and Crewe Works converted five HAAs and 81 HEAs into box-bodied mineral wagons to replace life-expired 21-ton coal wagons used for export traffic in South Wales and to supply cement works without hopper discharge equipment. MAA 392000, the first of the HAA conversions, is seen at Swansea Burrows Sidings in October 1994, while MEA 391068 was photographed at Ketton Cement works in October 1996.

ABOVE No more HAAs were converted but in 1995 a further 60 HEAs became MEAs, this batch being delivered in Mainline blue livery initially to work between Daw Mill Colliery and Rufford Stocking Site although by 1997 they had been transferred into a common nationwide pool together with all the other MEAs. M 391149 passes Peak Forest when carrying limestone from Dowlow Quarry to Ashburys in September 1999.

MIDDLE AND BOTTOM A fourth batch of 40 MEAs was converted at RFS, Doncaster for Loadhaul in 1996 while the success of the design, together with the virtual collapse of the domestic coal business, saw a further 490 HEAs converted into MEAs between 1996 and 2004. Loadhaul's 391211 and EWS-liveried 391623 were both recorded at Ketton in July 1998. Neither the Mainline nor the Loadhaul MEAs had the single end-ladder fitted to the other batches.

ABOVE Although there had been no more MAA conversions the rationalisation of the coal industry resulted in numerous HAAs becoming redundant and in 1997 some 400 were fitted with new low-height box-bodies and recoded MHA. Numbered 394001-400 they were intended for ballast and spoil traffic although in 1998 a pool of 30 were used to carry large granite boulders from Bardon Hill Quarry to Hessle, where the rocks were needed to protect the line near Ferriby from the encroaching River Humber. Note the revival of the COALFISH name as MHA 394144 waits to leave Bardon Hill in July 1998.

MIDDLE The growing requirement for air-braked engineers wagons also saw a number of MEAs being modified with cut-down bodies including 391131, photographed at Stoke in October 2000. The wagon has lost its 'M' prefix and been recoded MFA.

BOTTOM The 'MFA' code had previously been allocated to a pair of vehicles built in 1976 with underframes diverted from the HBA domestic coal hopper programme. Fitted with high-sided box-bodies, and a single side door to facilitate cleaning out, the two original MFAs initially carried scrap metal to the Sheerness Steel Co at Sheerness, but by 1982 they had both been fitted with a vacuum through pipe and recoded MFB for agricultural lime traffic from Ferryhill and Raisby to Burrelton and Inverurie. Subsequently they were briefly seen in coal traffic in South Wales before returning to steel scrap traffic in 1989 between Tube Investments, Chesterfield, and United Engineering Steel's Stocksbridge Works. In August 1991 MFB 390001, the second of the pair, was in store at Tees Yard and both would be withdrawn later that year.

ABOVE AND BELOW After the collapse of Tiger Rail in 1992 British Rail purchased their fleet of 182 two-axle POA and PNA two-axle mineral wagons. Renumbered and recoded ZKA they were assigned to the Civil Engineer with the name LIMPET, many having slots cut in the sides to prevent overloading when carrying spoil. However, in 1994 36 of the former Tiger Rail wagons were renumbered again, recoded MKA and returned to revenue service by Loadhaul to carry blending coal from Daw Mill Colliery and Killoch Washery. ZKA DC 390185 (formerly TRL 5481) is seen awaiting repair at Carlisle Currock in September 1993 while MKA 393009 (previously TRL 5254 and then ZKA DC 390222) was spotted deep in Mainline Freight territory at Toton whilst working between Daw Mill and Rufford in April 1995.

5
Covered Hoppers

ABOVE AND LEFT British Rail owned relatively few air-braked covered hoppers as many powdered commodities requiring protection from the elements were transported in privately owned wagons. However, in 1969 Shildon built a fleet of 52 two-axle 45-ton glw Covhops numbered 250000-51. Based on the MGR coal hopper and coded CBA they had automatic discharge gear with a capacity of 31 tons and initially carried lime from ICI's Tunstead Works to Port Talbot steelworks. In 1977 Shildon built five more CBAs, numbered 250052-56, to replace 250020/23/33/47/48 which had all been written off in a derailment at Chinley. Between 1984 and 1989 16 were hired by Cleveland Potash, being used to carry potash from Boulby to Ely, and rock salt from Boulby to Dundee and Ipswich, before the corrosive nature of these ladings resulted in their withdrawal. In 1990 the remaining CBAs were transferred to British Steel's own quarry at Hardendale, near Shap, from where they continued to supply Port Talbot with lime until withdrawal in 1999. CBA 250012 waits at Margam Yard in August 1991 while in May 1992 Valiant, an 0-6-0DH on hire from RFS Industries, shunts a rake of CBAs at Hardendale.

BELOW AND BOTTOM To replace its elderly vacuum-braked Clay Hoods and ensure the lucrative export flow of china clay through Fowey Docks remained on rail in 1988 BR agreed to build a fleet of replacement vehicles. Following the modification of HAA 353224 with a roller roof Doncaster Works built 124 new CDA wagons to this design numbered 375000-123, with an additional 14 CDAs, 375124-37 being converted from HAAs in 1989. All were delivered with an English China Clays logo on the side, although these were to wear off after several years in traffic. The large end vents facilitated unloading without the necessity to open the plastic sheeted top-cover. CDA 375008 is pictured at Fowey in July 1988 while CDA 375078 was spotted at Pontsmill in May 2001.

OPPOSITE TOP Doncaster Works also produced the CEAs when in 1996 they fitted roller roofs to 45 redundant HEAs on behalf of Loadhaul. With a capacity of 32 tons the CEAs were initially used to carry limestone from Tilcon's Rylstone Quarry to Leeds for construction of the A1/M1 link road before seeing a brief spell in coal traffic from Tees Dock to Blue Circle Cement at Hope. CEA 360878 is seen at Tees Yard in November 1998.

OPPOSITE BOTTOM By May 1999 the CEAs had been transferred to Cornwall to carry calcified seaweed fertiliser from Truro to Carlisle and china clay from Burngullow to the ECC terminal at Stoke Cliff Vale. Subsequently the type were used to carry shredded tyres and slag whilst in May 2000 CEA 361024 was recorded at Peak Forest after a trial in lime traffic from Hindlow.

ABOVE AND BELOW Pulverised fuel ash (PFA), more commonly known as fly ash, is an inevitable by-product from coal-fired power stations widely used by the construction industry and for land reclamation. In the 1960s BR built 412 fly ash wagons to handle workings from Drakelow 'C', Ratcliffe-on-Soar, and West Burton power stations, the first 206 fitted with vacuum brakes with capacities of either 17 or 21.5 tons while the other 206, built at Ashford between 1965 and 1968, were all 21.5 ton capacity vehicles fitted with air brakes. Coded CSA they worked to Fletton, where the PFA was used to fill old clay pits, and to terminals at Little Barford and Silvertown with ash for the construction industry. As the ash was blown out of the wagons by compressed air their design was based on the existing Presflo type, with two filling hatches atop each wagon and high-pressure air inlet and PFA/air outlet pipes situated on one side of the vehicle only. Following the closure of the Fletton site in 1991 and Little Barford in 1994 the CSAs were considered for a movement of fly ash from Longannet Power Station to the Blue Circle Cement plant at Westbury but with a maximum speed of 55mph they were eventually deemed unsuitable for this working and after a few years in store went to Booths of Rotherham for cutting up in 2000. In later years defective seals on the filling hatches, resulting in a loss of pressure when unloading, were an increasing problem and red and yellow squares were painted on the sides to help maintenance staff identify a particular filler. B 874086 is pictured at Peterborough in August 1992 while the view of B 874153, in store at Warrington in May 1997, shows the side with the discharge gear. *Mark Saunders (1)*

6

Flat Wagons

ABOVE AND LEFT A fleet of 2,122 bogie Freightliner flats fitted with 2ft 8in diameter wheels was built at Ashford and Shildon between 1964 and 1980. Comprising a skeletal framework they ran in semi-permanently coupled sets of up to five vehicles, while within each set there was no buffing gear, coupling being by means of a rigid bar with only the outer wagons having conventional buffers and draw-gear at one end. Initially the vehicles were fitted with Freightliner's own container fixings but soon after delivery it was recognised that ISO container fixing brackets were also required and from 1969 only ISO brackets were fitted to new builds. Each wagon could carry three 20ft containers or their equivalent, the 'Outers' coded FGA at 63ft 6in being a foot longer than the FFA 'Inners' to accommodate the buffing gear. Initially painted blue following refurbishment in the 1990s many were repainted black. FGA 601652 is pictured at Crewe Gresty Road in June 1997 while FFA 602160 was recorded at Crewe Basford Hall in June 2001.

TOP In 1981 the Standard Wagon Co built an experimental bogie skeletal conflat for the British Rail Research Department numbered RDB 998546 and coded YXA. Subsequently transferred to the revenue fleet becoming FGA 601995 the concept was to design a flat with reduced tare and lower building costs but by July 1995, after a few years evaluation in Freightliner traffic, it was to be found stored in Carlisle Kingmoor Yard.

MIDDLE In 1978 three FFAs, 602206/331/548, were fitted with through vacuum pipes and conventional buffing and draw-gear at both ends. Renumbered 601996-98 and recoded FJB they carried containers of general merchandise on behalf of Sutherland Transport running in mixed train formations between Aberdeen and Wick. When this service ended in 1985 they were transferred to other workings including calcium carbide from Immingham to Gartcosh, resin from Duxford to Stranraer and bulk whisky from the Chivas vatting plant at Keith to their bottling factory at Dalmuir Riverside. No longer requiring a vacuum pipe FJA 601997 was spotted at Mossend in July 1990.

BOTTOM Built at Ashford in 1966 with conventional draw-gear FJA 601999 also handled whisky from Keith but following the demise of Speedlink it was converted into an Auxiliary Hoist wagon for the S&T Department. Capable of carrying 24 equipment cabinets or point machines KDC 601999, recoded YSB, awaits attention at Chester Wagon shops in September 1995.

ABOVE AND BELOW The movement of containerised household waste from Greater London to disposal sites at Appleford, Calvert and Stewartby saw 150 former Freightliner flats being renumbered and reallocated to this traffic in 1977. The 90 inner wagons including 622909, photographed at Calvert with containers from Northolt in September 1991, were recoded FUA while the 60 outers became FYAs. Bringing up the rear of a Cricklewood to Stewartby train FYA 621515 is seen at Bedford in January 1990.

ABOVE In 1970 Ashford Works built an experimental 'Lowliner' for road vehicle traffic which consisted of five four-wheel flat wagons semi-permanently coupled together, while the following year it turned out two pairs of low-deck container flats, 699000/1 designated 'Lowliner A', and 699002/3 known as 'Lowliner B'. Each of the first pair of container vehicles was 42ft long with four-wheel bogies, while the 'Lowliner B' wagons were 62ft long with six-wheel bogies. Both sets had 2ft 4in diameter wheels giving a floor height of 2ft 10in compared to the 3ft 1in of standard Freightliner flats but they never went into series production. FHA 699002 is pictured at Cardiff Tidal Sidings in October 1990. *Hywel Thomas*

RIGHT However, the trend towards high-cube boxes, particularly in deep-sea container traffic, continued and in 1989 Powell Duffryn built a new three-part Lowliner set fitted with 520mm (approx 1ft 8in) diameter wheels capable of carrying 9ft 6in high containers on approved routes. Numbered PDUF 95090-92 the three vehicles were subsequently sold to BR becoming FLA set 606019/605028/606020 while BR also ordered an additional 27 inner and 18 outer FLAs from the Cardiff based manufacturer. Marshalled into nine five-wagon sets they initially operated a new service from the Isle of Grain to Willesden, a route with numerous loading gauge restrictions. Set 606013/6050 19/605020/605021/606014 passes Hoo Junction in October 1992.

THIS PAGE In 1993 the FLAs were released into general Freightliner traffic becoming a common sight on workings to and from the ports of Felixstowe and Southampton. Inner 605015, carrying a 40ft long, 9ft 6in high P&O Nedlloyd box is seen outside Containerbase at Barton Dock, Manchester in February 2005 while outer 606017 was spotted on the Barton Dock branch with an empty 8ft 6in Maersk Sealand box en route to Southampton in May 2006.

OPPOSITE PAGE The continued growth in container traffic saw BR purchase a new fleet of conventional bogie conflats from Arbel Fauvet in 1991. Built in France the order comprised 560 FSA outers and 140 FTA inners marshalled into two, three and four wagon sets which gave more flexibility to cope with varying traffic levels. FSA 608074 waits to leave Hull Docks in July 1992 with empty IFF powder containers, which were en route from Rotterdam to the ICI works at Wilton for reloading with nylon polymer, while FTA 607134 heads along the Barton Dock branch in April 1994 with a Gemstar box from Southampton.

LEFT In 1993 BR ordered 226 pairs of permanently coupled bogie 'Euro-Twin' container flats from Arbel Fauvet for Channel Tunnel traffic. Coded FIA each set could carry two 40ft or 45ft or four 20ft containers or the equivalent 13.6m or 7.82m swap-bodies or a combination thereof. FIA set 31 70 4938 144-3 leaves Willesden with Hoyer tank containers from Trafford Park en route to Duisberg in June 1998.

ABOVE 'Euro-Twin' sets assigned to ACI (Allied Continental Intermodal) service were delivered in a bright green livery, FIA 31 70 4938 124-5 being recorded passing Didcot in a special working from Cardiff to Turin in October 1994. However, this colour would quickly disappear beneath a layer of brake dust and grime.

LEFT In 1966 Ashford built three 25-ton two-axle container flats, with a further 20 constructed at Shildon the following year. Numbered 511000-22, with 2ft 8in diameter wheels and a 3ft 3in high deck, all were initially allocated to Irish Shipping Services traffic via Heysham and Holyhead but by the 1970s they were carrying boxes of car parts from Cowley to Harwich and bulk whisky from north-east Scotland to bottling plants around Glasgow. FBB 511008 is pictured at Mossend en route to Dalmuir Riverside in June 1990.

ABOVE In the 1960s and 1970s BR converted over 900 redundant coach underframes into Carflats fitting them with wooden floors and low side rails. Many were vacuum-braked but amongst the dual-braked Carflats were a batch of 20 converted from ex-Stanier LMS 60ft underframes at Derby in 1966 which included FVX B 745847, photographed at Eastleigh in October 1987.

BELOW Between 1976 and 1979 BR also converted 15 Freightliner flats into commercial vehicle carriers, initially for traffic from the British Leyland factory at Bathgate, fitting them with wooden floors and bridging plates between vehicles. Recoded FMA they were marshalled in three-wagon sets, each with ramped ends, and in later years could be seen in Ford traffic from Southampton as well as occasionally carrying soft-topped military vehicles between Ashchurch, Ludgershall and Marchwood. FMA set 602036/60/71, loaded with Ford Transits for Wakefield, passes Eastleigh in September 1989.

7
Two-axle Steel Carriers

ABOVE Based on the experience gained from B 920500, a prototype two-axle steel wagon built in 1966, four year later Ashford Works constructed a fleet of 300 31-ton capacity, 45ton glw, Steel ABs numbered 400000-299. Unlike the earlier vehicle they had no sides but retained the low drop-down ends and swivel side stanchions while the floor was fitted with eight 4in turnover bolsters. However, they were quickly superseded in steel traffic by the Bogie Steel ABs and relegated to use as barrier and runner wagons. Having lost its ends when reassigned as a runner the former SAB (the first 57 Steel ABs had a through vacuum pipe, the rest being coded SAA) 400031 now recoded RRB is pictured at British Steel's Shelton Works, Etruria in June 1994.

LEFT In 1974 42 Steel ABs were fitted with floor spigots and a tool box at one end to carry sheeted coils of tinplate (the sheets and spare spigots being stored in the tool box until required) from the British Steel tinplate works at Ebbw Vale, Trostre and Velindre to the Metal Box factories at Sutton-in-Ashfield, Westhoughton and Wisbech. Loaded with three 10-ton tinplate coils 400188, recoded KTA, was spotted at Whitemoor Yard in June 1980. *Trevor Mann*

TOP In 1984 170 Steel ABs were converted at Derby and Doncaster Works into FPA container flats. Intended to serve coal depots not equipped to handle hopper wagons they were introduced during the miners strike and initially carried containerised rock salt from Cheshire to Scotland and Southern England. In coal traffic they regularly worked from South Wales and FPA 400065 passes Cardiff Pengam en route from Coedbach Washery to Inverness coal depot in July 1990.

MIDDLE AND BELOW Other commodities handled by the FPAs included dolofines from Thrislington Quarry to Gartcosh, sugar beet pulp nuts from Cantley and South Lynn to Glasgow Shieldhall, and slag from Lackenby to Mossend and Scunthorpe. Containers of dolofines (a type of limestone) destined for Ravenscraig steelworks are seen being unloaded at Gartcosh in July 1987 while FPA 400270 was recorded at Tees Yard with a sheeted container of slag consigned to the North East Slag Cement Co of Scunthorpe in April 1998.

ABOVE AND BELOW A less successful conversion took place in 1986 when four Steel ABs, 400042/120/244/97, were adapted to each carry four small 'Minilink' containers which could be loaded on and off from the side by a similarly equipped road lorry. Recoded FBA the four wagons operated between Glasgow Shieldhall and Willesden but the concept, which had been aimed at the movement of low-volume high-value merchandise, never took off and by 1991 all were stored at Carlisle Currock. FBA 400042 is seen at Warrington Arpley in November 1986 while 400120 was being unloaded at Shieldhall that same month.

OPPOSITE PAGE In 1977 Ashford rebuilt two Steel ABs into prototype plate wagons with fixed ends and four drop-doors each side, although when the new type, coded SPA, went into full scale production at Shildon in 1979 they only had three doors per side. Numbered 460002-461101 the Shildon built SPAs were fitted with Bruninghaus springs and, delivered in flame red livery, they proved most versatile, handling various sorts of semi-finished steel. SPA 460387 loaded with bundles of short steel billets from Stocksbridge Steelworks passes Tinsley Yard en route to Tube Investments at Chesterfield in July 1985 while 461088, loaded with coiled bar from BSC's Parkgate & Rawmarsh Works for export to Scandinavia, is seen at Immingham in October 1990.

ABOVE, LEFT AND BELOW In 1983 35 SPA were recoded SHA after being fitted with a tool box and coil spigots to replace the KTAs in tinplate traffic from South Wales, 461010 being recorded at Warrington C&W in March 1986, while another 80 SPAs were modified by replacing the doors with a sloping side rail. Initially recoded KOA this was amended to SKA in 1984, the wagons being used to carry rod coil from the Allied Steel & Wire mills at Cardiff and Scunthorpe although by 1995 all were out of use. Empty SKA 461004 is pictured at Scunthorpe in May 1987 while a sheeted 460567 waits to leave Cardiff for Mossend in May 1991.

TOP To provide the rod coil with better protection from the elements 35 SPAs were fitted with 'Slideflex' hoods in 1988 and recoded SEA. They also operated from Cardiff Rod Mill and SEA 461100 was destined to the Cobra freight depot at Wakefield when photographed at Tees Yard in June 1991. Such circuitous routings were not uncommon at this date as the Metals Sector aimed to reduce costs by accommodating as much traffic as possible on its own dedicated trains, rather than utilise the soon to close Speedlink network.

MIDDLE In 1997 24 of the redundant SKAs were fitted with coil cradles to handle imports of stainless steel from the USA. Initially they ran from Liverpool Docks to Avesta Steel at Panteg but from 1998, when they were recoded SCA, they could also be found carrying imported coils for annealing at BSC's Ebbw Vale Works. A rake of SCAs heads for Ebbw Vale through the outskirts of Newport in February 2001.

BELOW A pool of 40 SPAs fitted with wooden cradles in 1984 could also be found in imported coil traffic operating from the East Coast ports of Grimsby, Immingham and Killingholme, 460595 being recorded at Warrington Dallam Freight Depot with two coils from Grimsby Docks in May 1986.

TOP Although standard SPAs could be used to carry steel slabs in 1986 Immingham C&W converted 30 into SDAs by removal of the doors and the installation of three bolsters. This facilitated their unloading by fork lift and they were used to carry steel slabs from BSC Scunthorpe to Rotherham Masborough from where the slabs were roaded to McCalls in Brynsworth. SDA 460706 was awaiting maintenance at Thornaby C&W when spotted at Tees Yard in July 1995.

MIDDLE In 1982 330 SPAs were transferred to the Civil Engineer as general material carriers and given the engineers fleet name PIKE. Recoded ZAA DC 460177 was carrying a scrap bogie when recorded at Crewe Gresty Lane in October 1999.

BOTTOM In 1989 three HEAs, 360040/761/1486, were rebuilt as scrap wagons with box bodies and recoded SJA. Initially found on workings to Cardiff and Llanwern they subsequently worked from Tube Investments, Chesterfield and T. J. Thomson at Stockton to the UES (United Engineering Steel) plants at Aldwarke and Deepcar, before all three were transferred to internal use at Aldwarke in 1996. SJA 361486 was recorded at Tees Yard in June 1993.

TOP The 181 Railease 51-ton glw POA scrap wagons were purchased by BR in 1990 and renumbered 470000-180. Recoded SSA the majority remained in steel scrap traffic to UES but 40 were reassigned to coal traffic including blending flows from Blindwells and Wardley and the movement of coal slurry from Killoch and Westfield. The coal slurry was burnt at Methil Power Station where SSAs 470110 (ex-RLS 5910) and 470149 (ex-RLS 5949) were recorded in May 1993.

RIGHT AND BELOW In 1996 several SSAs were repainted in Transrail grey including 470158 photographed at Tees Yard that September, but the following year all were re-bodied prior to a return to scrap traffic. SSA 470035 illustrates the more substantial body as fitted by EWS when spotted at Tees Yard in March 1998.
Mark Saunders (1)

THIS PAGE AND OPPOSITE Six redundant SKAs were converted at Chester Wagon Shops in 1994 into a Tunnel Inspection Train. All were recoded ZDA, DC 460484 and DC 460606 being fitted with a dual-height platform, DC 461087 having a full-height platform, while the other three DC 460743, DC 460815 and DC 461079 became Access/Accommodation/Water Tank vehicles respectively. All bar DC 460606, which was identical to DC 460484, are illustrated at Chester in April 1995. The Tunnel Inspection Train also included former BR Ferry Van DB 787297 (see page 30, bottom pic).

8 Bogie Steel Carriers

ABOVE Some 305 air-braked Bogie Steel wagons numbered 900000-198/200-305 were built at Ashford and Shildon between 1972 and 1976. Rated at 102 tonnes glw with a tare of 24.5 tonnes and mounted on FBT6 bogies they were 40ft long and had high ends, the details of which varied between lots, while the floor comprised a series of transverse 'U' channel sections with reinforcing mesh between ensuring rapid heat dissipation when loaded with hot steel products. Coded BAA or BAB the Bogie Steel ABs often carried steel coil, loaded either 'Eye-to-Sky' or on the roll, and BAB 900047 had been fitted with wooden cradles when spotted at Kings Lynn in September 1986 with imported coil destined for Brierley Hill.

LEFT In 1978 over 60 Bogie Steel ABs were fitted with low profile coil cradles and recoded BKA or BKB earning the nickname 'Kinky Beam' wagons, although by 1985 they had all reverted back to their original BAA or BAB coding whilst still retaining the coil cradles. BAB 900014, loaded with coils of 'Chequerplate', was en route from Lackenby to Blackburn when photographed at Warrington in April 1985.

ABOVE Over 100 Bogie Steel ABs had more substantial cradles capable of accommodating larger diameter coils and in 1992 these were recoded BZA. The majority worked from Lackenby steelworks but a pool of eight were assigned to Grimsby and Immingham Docks for the carriage of imported stainless steel coils to the Avesta works in Sheffield. BZA 900282, one of the final series of Bogie Steel ABs built at Ashford in 1976, is seen at Grimsby in October 1995. On this batch the bogies were centred at 26ft 3in in contrast to 26ft 6in for the earlier vehicles while the web of the side at 21in was 4in deeper and they also had higher ends.

BELOW As not all customers wished to receive their coil loaded 'Gunshot' fashion, that is 'Eye-to-End', a number of wagons had side facing cradles while in 1994, 24 were fitted with a combination of two transverse facing and three longitudinal facing cradles. Recoded BXA they also worked from Grimsby, 900256 loaded with one 10 ton and two 20 ton coils being recorded in July 1995.

ABOVE AND BELOW Following a further rearrangement of their cradles in 1996 all 24 BXAs were recoded BSA. Repainted in Loadhaul livery BSA 900032 waits to leave Grimsby Dock with imported coils for Sheffield in October 1995 while BSA 900196 is seen being loaded at Immingham Dock in August 1996 with coil destined for Wolverhampton Steel Terminal.

ABOVE Early in 1994 the British Steel works in South Wales informed BR of their wish to load all coil 'bore horizontal' as this method of handling reduced damage. Consequently 55 BAAs and 265 BBAs had the floors replaced by three 'Coil Boxes' which enabled them to carry larger coils than could be accommodated on existing cradles. All worked from Llanwern and Port Talbot to the galvanising plant at Shotton and the tinplate works at Ebbw Vale and Trostre. One of the former BAAs 900103, now coded BCA, is seen at Margam Yard in October 1994.

MIDDLE To handle 'bright steel', which required protection from the elements, BAA 900160 was fitted with an experimental Structureflex hood at Cardiff Cathays Wagon Shops in 1985. Subsequently a variant of the design was adopted by Powell Duffryn for its own fleet of covered coil carriers and 900160 worked alongside the privately-owned wagons carrying cold reduced coil from Hamworthy Dock and Port Talbot to the Leyland car body plant in Swindon and steel stockholders in the West Midlands. It is seen at Margam C&W in September 1990.

BOTTOM Another two BAAs, 900219 and 900257, were fitted with weatherproof hoods in 1991 for coil traffic from Boston and Grimsby. Recoded BKA 900257 is pictured at Middlesbrough Goods in September 1995.

LEFT AND BELOW In 1973 Shildon built a prototype BBA with a further 690, numbered 910001-365/367-691, being constructed at Ashford between 1974 and 1980. They weighed 27 tonnes with a carrying capacity of 75 tonnes and were 10ft longer than the BAAs with deeper side frames. A similar channel floor provided for the carriage of semi-finished steel products and BBA 910270, loaded with five hot rolled coils destined for Shotton, is pictured at Margam in April 1992 while the partially unloaded 910075 is seen at British Steel's Shelton Works on June 5, 1994, having arrived earlier in the week with steel blooms from Lackenby.

LEFT The final 150 BBAs had lifting lugs that protruded from the solebar over each bogie as illustrated by 910578, one of a handful repainted with yellow ends. Photographed at Tees Yard in February 1991 it was one of 172 BBAs assigned to Lackenby for the carriage of steel blooms to the British Steel works at Shelton and Workington and steel slab to the plate mill at Dalzell.

ABOVE AND BELOW In the 1970s BR began transporting stainless steel slabs from BSC's SMACC (Stainless Melting and Continuous Casting) Works at Tinsley Park, Sheffield to Lackenby for rolling into coil, the coils then being returned to Sheffield for finishing at BSC's SPACE (Stainless Plate and Coil Expansion) Works. To handle this two-way traffic 35 BBAs had their ends removed and six low coil cradles fitted, the slabs resting on top of the cradles for the journey north, and in June 1986 two of the modified BBAs together with four BDAs all loaded with slab for Lackenby, were recorded at Tinsley Yard. Stainless steel slabs were also railed from Sheffield to Grimsby Dock from where they were shipped to Germany, Holland and Sweden for rolling and by 1993 standard BBAs and BDAs were handling this traffic. BBA 910183 waits unloading at Grimsby in October 1995.

ABOVE By 1995 13 of the endless BBAs, now with just five cradles and recoded BWA, were amongst the various types in coil traffic from Grimsby Dock, BWA 910450 being recorded on 31 October. The wagon had been stopped by the local Loads Examiner since it had been loaded with one coil that broke the '2/3rds Rule' which required that 'the width across the cradle at the points of contact should not be less than two-thirds of the outside diameter of the coil'. Later that day 910450 would be shunted back to the quayside where the coil could be transferred to a BSA wagon fitted with the larger 30-ton cradles.

MIDDLE In 1995 a dozen BBAs were fitted with cradles removed from the withdrawn fleet of BOA coil carriers. Recoded BIA all 12 were painted in Loadhaul livery and on the morning of October 9, 1995 BIA 910504 was one of 36 loaded coil wagons to be found at Grimsby all destined for the SPACE works in Sheffield.

BOTTOM To work alongside the BCAs in coil traffic from Llanwern and Port Talbot 265 BBAs were fitted with coil boxes in 1994. Recoded BLA 910086 is seen at Dee Marsh Sidings, Shotton in July 1996.

ABOVE The prototype BBA 910000 was recoded BUA in 1991 after modification to carry hot slabs from the SMACC works in Sheffield to Lackenby. Photographed at Tinsley Yard in May 1992 it became known as the 'Hot Coffin', having a new plate floor and steel cover lined with refractory bricks in which to transport a stainless steel slab at up to 800^{0}c (the normal maximum temperature for loading steel onto railway wagons being 450^{0}c). The slabs were of a special type that could not fall below 500^{0}c without becoming brittle but unfortunately the insulation proved insufficient and after just three or four loaded trips the BUA was withdrawn. *David Larkin*

BELOW Subsequently the BUA, along with the BIAs and BWAs, were all converted into covered coil carriers by EWS with three telescopic sliding hoods primarily to handle imports of bright steel from the East Coast ports to steel stockholders in the West Midlands. All would eventually be recoded BXA including 910307, previously a BWA, spotted at Tees Yard in August 1998.

ABOVE In 1975 two existing unfitted 30-ton capacity Bogie Bolster Cs were fitted with air brakes and Y25 bogies at Swindon Works and recoded BCA. Subsequently allocated to the engineers' fleet the first of the pair ADC 960000, now recoded YVA, is pictured at Bescot in May 1990.

BELOW Between 1975 and 1979 1,251 unfitted Bogie Bolster Ds were rebuilt with air brakes at Ashford and Shildon. Apart from 950000, which only had five bolsters, the rest were fitted with six, although from 950501 the bolster design was modified with steel sections topped by a wooden rubbing strip replacing all timber construction. At 52ft long they carried 57 tonnes and BDA 950378 was loaded with sheeted steel section from Shelton when recorded at Immingham in August 1990.

OPPOSITE TOP AND MIDDLE Over 250 BDAs were recoded YAA after transfer to the Engineers in 1983 and given the code-name BRILL. DC 950842 is pictured at Tees Yard in September 1995 with new rail from Workington destined for export to India via Tees Dock. The final 450 BDAs, numbered 950801-951250, had bogie mounted wheel handbrakes instead of the single hand lever brake found on each side of the earlier conversions. Tees Dock also handled the export of steel section and BDA 950644, repainted in Loadhaul livery earlier that year, had just arrived from Lackenby's 10in Beam Mill with section destined for Singapore when photographed on 2 November 1996.

OPPOSITE BOTTOM When wagons carried an overhanging load they would often be accompanied by runner wagons but a 'runner' was not required if the load did not project more than 450mm beyond the headstock. However, wagons with overhanging loads could not be coupled together with the overhanging portions adjacent to each other when either overhang was greater than 300mm. BDA 950786 waits to leave Shelton Steelworks with section for Tees Dock in June 1994.

TOP Eighty BDAs were recoded BFA in 1986 after fitting with a higher end bolster to facilitate two-tier loading of steel billet. The BFAs initially worked from Scunthorpe Steelworks to Rotherham Masborough Freight Depot from where the billet was roaded to BSC's Templeborough Works. Lettered 'BSC SCUNTHORPE' BFA 950633 waits unloading at Rotherham in October 1995.

MIDDLE In the 1990s a pool of 20 BDAs were assigned to convey aluminium ingots from the smelter at Lynemouth to Wolverhampton Steel Terminal from where they were delivered by road to the Alcan rolling mill at Rogerstone. BDA 950229 loaded with five 10-ton ingots is pictured at Tees Yard in January 1998.

BOTTOM Nine YAAs returned to the revenue fleet in 1988 to assist with the movement of timber brought down by the severe storms of the previous year. Modified with high stanchions they initially worked from Ashford, Chichester and Crawley to Blackburn and Shrewsbury, DC 950099 repainted in Railfreight Distribution's red and grey livery, being recorded at Warrington in August 1988. Subsequently recoded BTA they remained in timber traffic until 1992 when they were returned to the Engineers or were rebuilt as BMA wagons.

ABOVE The BTA code was reissued in 1997 when 31 BDAs were converted into pipe carriers by EWS to transport both 18in and 20in pipes from Hartlepool Tube Works to Laurencekirk. With six channel stanchions each side they could carry up to 15 pipes compared to only 10 if loaded onto a conventional BDA. BTA 950668 waits to leave Tees Yard in April 1998.

BELOW In 1990 three YAAs were modified to carry the six Bridge Beam wagons DW 84997, DW 85000 and DB 998070-73 that, because of their heavy springing, were not permitted to move on their own wheels when empty as there was a danger of derailment on a curve. Recoded YXA the former Bogie Bolsters replaced a pool of six SPA plate wagons in this role. DC 950153, loaded with 'Conger' wagons DB 998072 and DB 998073, is seen at Bescot Open Day in May 1990.

LEFT Eighty unfitted Boplate were air-braked and fitted with Y25C bogies at Shildon in 1980/81 and renumbered 965000-79. At 52ft long with a capacity of 58 tons they were initially used to carry steel plate from Scunthorpe primarily to shipyards, but with the decline in British ship-building by the mid-1980s five had been reassigned to carry ingots from BSC's River Don Works in Sheffield to Ravenscraig while another 10 had been transferred to the rod coil traffic from Scunthorpe. BPA 965058 waits unloading at Warrington Dallam in August 1986.

ABOVE In 1981/82 Shildon rebuilt 150 Borail wagons with air brakes and Y25CSS bogies so that the movement of new rail from Workington steelworks could be transferred to the Speedlink network. Numbered 967500-649 the 49-ton capacity BRAs were fitted with six new bolsters as well as very low ends and sides, which were cut into at six places where the tensioners for the webbing straps were located. Transferred to the Civil Engineer in 1983 and recoded YLA, with the code name MULLET, DC 967515 is pictured at Castleton Long-Welded Rail Depot with a load of new rail from Workington in April 1986.

LEFT In addition to rails the 62ft long YLAs handled other lengthy loads such as concrete bridge beams and plastic pipes while in 1995 six were assigned to Allied Steel & Wire for the carriage of 60ft reinforcing bar from Cardiff to Mossend and Warrington. DC 967606 waits unloading at Warrington Dallam in October 1995.

ABOVE In 1990 69 YLAs were recoded YQA and named PARR after having their bolsters removed to enable them to carry new concrete sleepers from the Costain factory at Coltness. YQA DC 967560 was photographed at Warrington when en route to Crewe Gresty Lane Pre-Assembly Depot in September 1991.

BELOW Twelve prototype 90-tonne glw steel carriers were built to three different lengths by RFS Industries, Doncaster, in 1990; all of which could be fitted with a 'Slideflex' hood if required. Shortest were the four BGAs numbered 961000-3, which at 13m long could carry 64 tonnes, and 961000 was recorded at Tees Yard with coil in May 2002.

TOP The next four prototype steel carriers, numbered 962000-3 and coded BHA, were 16m long with a payload of 60.5 tonnes and like the BGAs could accommodate steel coils up to 2m diameter in the well recessed between the bogies. However, despite the designs being the result of an collaboration between RFS and BR the wagons were unpopular with ground staff, the high ends proving to be a particular inconvenience during loading and unloading. BHA 962000 waits to leave Middlesbrough Goods with cold reduced coil for Wolverhampton Steel Terminal in September 1995.

ABOVE The last four prototypes were the 19m long BJAs intended for steel bar and section traffic but again their high ends proved problematic and 963000-3 saw little use other than a brief spell carrying rebar from Cardiff. BJA 963000 is pictured out of use at Tees Yard in June 1991.

OPPOSITE TOP The 20 dual-braked Bogie Coil Ks were converted at Swindon in 1966 from a batch of 1961 built vacuum-braked slab wagons. In addition to air-brakes they gained two large coil cradles, one 7ft 3¼in long and the other 14ft 1¼in, each covered with its own sideways folding nylon hood supported by three tarpaulin bars. Initially coded JKX they worked from the steelworks at Gartcosh, Llanwern, Port Talbot and Shotton while in 1976 10 became JIXs after being ferry-fitted to handle coil traffic to the Continent via the Dover Train Ferry. All were recoded BNX in 1983 by which date six were to be found working from Hamworthy Docks with imported cold reduced coil for the Pressed Steel works in Swindon. B 949537 passes Eastleigh station in October 1986.

OPPOSITE BOTTOM In 1991, having had their hoods removed, 16 BNXs were assigned to Grimsby primarily to carry the massive 35-ton coils that could not be accommodated on other air-braked wagon types. Repainted in Railfreight red and black B 949512 waits to leave Grimsby Dock with coil for Sheffield in October 1995.

9
Specials, Departmental Wagons and Brake Vans

ABOVE AND LEFT Although they were bogie steel carriers the 51 air-braked Trestles, numbered 990000-50, were classed as Special Wagons. Converted from vacuum-braked Trestles at Ashford and Shildon between 1977 and 1979, and fitted with Y25C bogies, they carried wide steel plate loaded at an angle that would have fouled the loading gauge if carried flat. Initially coded XVA they became BXAs in 1984 when the 'X' classification for special wagons was dropped and worked from Scunthorpe's heavy plate mill to shipyards and steel stockholders around the country. Regular destinations included the Swan Hunter yards at Carville, Hebburn and Wallsend and Austin & Pickersgill in Sunderland but, by 1986, British Steel had standardised on the manufacture of 2m wide plate, which could be loaded flat, and after a short period out of use the BXAs were reassigned to barrier wagon duty or converted into runner wagons. BXA 990013 was one of 10 in store at Tinsley Yard when photographed in December 1986, while 990034 had lost all its bodywork and become an RRA runner when recorded passing through Oxford in June 1989.

TOP In 1990 all 51 former BXAs were converted into coil carriers and recoded BOA. Fitted with five cradles they initially worked from Ravenscraig before being transferred to the East Coast ports. Sporting a Metals Sector logo and loaded with imported coil destined for Brierley Hill, BOA 990004 waits to leave Grimsby in March 1991. However, the BOAs were not a success as rough loading with heavy coils resulted in bent frames and by 1996 all had either been withdrawn or converted back to runners.

MIDDLE Another fleet of vacuum-braked special wagons to be air-braked were the 24 Flatrol MJs built at Swindon in 1963 to carry irradiated nuclear fuel from the CEGB's Magnox power stations to the British Nuclear Fuels Ltd reprocessing plant at Sellafield. In 1980 their original six-wheel plate-back bogies were replaced with air-braked four-wheel FBT6M bogies, while at the same time the wagon frames were strengthened to enable them to carry the heavier flasks forwarded by Britain's second generation of nuclear power stations, the Advanced Gas-Cooled Reactors. Having been recoded from XKV to XKB in 1980 their code was further amended to FNB in 1984, around the time they were fitted with sliding covers. First of the fleet B 900509, having lost its through vacuum pipe, passes Warrington Bank Quay en route from Bridgwater to Sellafield (with a flask from Hinckley Point Power Station) in August 1986.

BOTTOM In 1970 Shildon built six nuclear flask wagons, numbered 550000-5, that were fitted with Gloucester bogies and air-braked from new. Known as Flatrol MJJs at 37ft long they were almost 12ft shorter than the Flatrol MJs and consequently required barrier wagons between themselves and the locomotive and Brake Van. Coded XKB they remained in main-line traffic until 1987 and 550004 is pictured at Warrington Walton Old Junction in February 1982. As the flask had been fitted with a shock absorber, the sunshield has been stored on the end platform of the wagon. *Trevor Mann*

LEFT AND BELOW The next six Flatrol MJJs, numbered 550009-14 and built at Ashford in 1976, were to a radical new design having Y25C bogies and an unpainted stainless steel body to facilitate decontamination. Between 1978 and 1986 the BREL workshops at Ashford, Shildon and Swindon built another dozen similar Flatrol MJJs while a final batch of 34 was constructed at Procor's Horbury Works in 1988, although unlike the earlier vehicles these were delivered without a through vacuum pipe, but with a sliding cover from new. XKB 550014 is seen at Warrington in April 1980 carrying an AGR flask fitted with a shock absorber collar while FNA 550059, the penultimate wagon, was recorded at Sellafield in May 2005. *Trevor Mann* (1)

BELOW BR built relatively few air-braked departmental wagons, as by the early 1980s there were a sufficient number of redundant revenue vehicles available for transfer to the Engineers. Furthermore, it was decided to air brake existing unfitted wagons including six 12-ton drop-side opens which were modified in 1978 for use as general material carriers on the underground Merseyrail Loop in Liverpool. Code named SOLE ZCA DB 982197 awaits repair at Chester C&W in April 1995.

BELOW In 1979 Shildon began converting five vacuum-braked Bogie Bolster Es into air-braked two-axle steel carriers but after work had commenced the order was cancelled. However, the underframes had already been equipped with FAT23 Taperlite suspension and in 1983 two entered service as Match Wagons with the Eastern Region's single-line ballast cleaners while the other three, coded ZCA, were fitted with a low-sided body complete with end plates. Code named POLLOCK DB 924820 was recorded at Eastleigh in May 1995.

TOP In 1982/83 Shildon also built three departmental open wagons, a single two-axle vehicle code named CARP and two bogie vehicles known as HALIBUT. Coded YCA the 56 tonne bogie opens were built with angled end plates but these had been removed by June 1994 when DB 981001, the second of the pair, was photographed at Immingham Reception Sidings.

RIGHT In 1988 Doncaster Works air-braked 30 20 ton two-axle GRAMPUS, fitting them with roller bearings and replacing their part removable, part hinged ends, with solid ends. Renamed RUDD they remained in general departmental traffic, ZBA DB 985879 being recorded at Radyr in August 1991.

BELOW Then in 1990/91 another 800 RUDD were introduced although these utilised the underframes from former 21-ton coal hoppers that were fitted with new bodies and air brakes. Numbered DB 97200-799 the conversion work was split between Marcroft Engineering, Stoke and CC Crump at Connahs Quay. Assigned to the Liverpool Division ZBA DB 972069 was sporting a Liver Bird motif on the side when photographed at Chester in May 1994.

ABOVE Numbered DB 982350-439 the 50 tonne capacity WHALE were the first air-braked bogie ballast hoppers being built at Shildon in 1966/67. Coded YHA at 40ft long they were initially assigned to the Southern Region before being transferred to the North West in the early 1980s. DB 982436 is pictured at St Helens Shaw Street in April 1985.

LEFT AND BELOW Based on a design introduced by the Southern Railway in 1928 BR's fleet of 40 tonne capacity ballast hoppers were somewhat shorter at 33ft 10in over headstocks. Built at Shildon and Ashford between 1971 and 1982 this fleet comprised 460 dual-braked SEALION numbered DB 982440-539 and DB 982568-927, together with 279 air-braked/vacuum-piped SEACOW. Like the SEALION the first batch of SEACOW, DB 982540-67, also had Gloucester bogies while the others, numbered DB 980000-250, were fitted with the type Y27CS. YGH DB 982604 is seen at Rugby in July 2000 while YGB DB 980135 was recorded at Stoke Cockshute Ballast Sidings in April 1990.

OPPOSITE TOP In 1991 a programme commenced to fit lights to over 200 YGB/YGHs while five SEACOW and 27 SEALION were equipped with generators to provide the power. All 32 were renamed STINGRAY and Transrail liveried DB 980172 is seen at Peak Forest in August 1999.

OPPOSITE BOTTOM To accompany the air-braked hoppers over 30 vacuum-braked Ballast Plough Vans, known as SHARK, had been fitted with air pipes by the late 1980s, while in the 1990s 20 were equipped with air brakes and a through vacuum pipe including ZUB DB 993826 recorded at Tees Yard in February 1999.

ABOVE AND BELOW A single air-braked prototype bogie rail wagon, coded YMA, was built at Shildon in 1983 but DB 996699 was to remain a one-off as BR decided to air brake over 600 of its existing fleet of unfitted SALMON which most commonly were used to transport 60ft track panels. The unique DB 996699, loaded with switch rail, is seen at Scunthorpe Freight Depot in October 1995 while one of the converted vehicles YMA DB 996591, built in 1957 with plate-back bogies, was recorded at Chester C&W six months earlier.

ABOVE AND BELOW BR also fitted air brakes to over 300 of its 66ft long sleeper wagons that were based on an LNER design with a low floor, removable ends and either hinged or drop-sides. Initially known as STURGEON DB 994123 had been recoded YPA and renamed TENCH when photographed at Crewe Gresty Lane in September 1997. The STURGEON name was retained by those wagons that had their sides and ends removed such as YFA DB 994270, photographed at Chester C&W in June 1993. Fitted with two sets of lift gear for loading/unloading rail its pale green livery indicated that the wagon was assigned to 'Operation Clean Sweep', a local initiative to remove discarded sleepers, rails and concrete troughing from the railways right of way.

OPPOSITE PAGE In 1981 Ashford Works built 22 SKATE wagons for a new Skip Train designed to work with a ballast-cleaning machine. Its design allowed the loading of spoil to be confined to the single track being cleaned without the need to occupy the adjacent line, the skips being carried along the length of the train by a travelling gantry. Numbered DB 997801-22 each wagon could accommodate seven small skips and the train was spotted at work near Kennett in July 1988. However, the concept did not catch on outside the Eastern Region and the wagons were withdrawn and cut up at Healey Mills in March 1995.

TOP AND MIDDLE More widespread were the Long Welded Rail trains built by Cowans Sheldon and Plasser & Theurer in 1986 which were designed to deliver lengths of LWR from the rail welding depots at Castleton and Eastleigh to relaying sites across the country. One wagon within each train was equipped with a small power unit, to enable movement within the work site without tying up a locomotive, while a small control cabin was fitted to one of the end wagons. DB 979508 is seen at Castleton in April 1986 whilst loaded YEA DB 979012 was spotted at Didcot in May 2005.

BOTTOM Although the advent of the air-braked wagon fleet hastened the demise of the Brake Van a significant number were retained for specific workings and, commencing in 1968, over 200 vacuum-piped Brake Vans were additionally equipped with an air pipe and gauge. Such Brake Vans were initially distinguished by the painting of yellow panels on the veranda screens and on either side of the ducket, as well as being lettered 'AIR PIPED', while the TOPS code was amended from CAP to CAR. B 954816 had also been branded 'FOR USE WITH AIR/BRAKE TRAINS ONLY' when recorded at Wigan Springs Branch in April 1985.

LEFT Many dual-piped Brake Vans were repainted into Railfreight red and grey livery in the 1980s including B 955101, photographed at Tees Yard in February 1992. Lettered 'REDMIRE TRAFFIC ONLY' it was coupled to the rear of the daily stone train that ran from Redmire to British Steel's Redcar Works, a Brake Van being necessary to accommodate the guard who had to close numerous crossing gates following the passage of the train along the branch line between Redmire and Northallerton.

MIDDLE AND BELOW Until the mid-1990s a Brake Van was required at the rear of any train conveying nuclear flasks or poisonous gases, so that in the event of an accident the guard would be in a position to go back along the line to carry out train protection without having to walk past the wagons, while one was also often marshalled at the rear of a train that had to perform a lenghty propelling move such as between the UKF Fertiliser depot at Akeman Street and the junction with the Claydon to Aylesbury line at Grendon Underwood Junction. CAR B 954997 waits its next turn of duty at Akeman Street in September 1991. This was one of 10 Brake Vans that had previously been used with the REAs to accompany the movement of London Underground stock, hence this complimentary repaint, while in the 1990s several Brake Vans were repainted in the new dark grey livery. However, their use continued to decline and CAR B 954758 was awaiting the cutters torch when photographed at Norton's scrap yard, Trafford Park in August 1992.